3/09

Brett Favre

by Michael Sandler

Consultant: Norries Wilson
Head Football Coach, Columbia University

BEARPORT
PUBLISHING

New York, New York

Credits

Cover, © Lucas Jackson/Reuters/Landov; Title Page, © Andy Manis/Bloomberg News/Landov; 4, © Tim Isbell/The Sun Herald/MCT/Landov; 5, © Jonathan Daniel/Allsport/Getty Images; 6, © Vernon Biever/NFL Photos/Getty Images; 7, © Andy Hayt/Getty Images; 8, © Tim Isbell/ The Sun Herald/MCT/Landov; 9, © Ronald C. Modra/Sports Illustrated/Getty Images; 10, © Allen Steele/Getty Images; 11, © Allen Steele/Getty Images; 12, © Al Messerschmidt/NFL/ Getty Images; 13, © NFL/WireImage/Newscom; 14, © AP Images/Lanny Ignelzi; 15, © Gary Hershorn/Reuters/Landov; 16, Courtesy of Cathy Dworak/Packers.com; 17, © Courtesy of Green Bay Miracle League/Michelle Lemmens; 18, © Courtesy of Gaits to Success; 19, © AP Images/Nicole LaCour Young; 20, © William Perlman/Star Ledger/Corbis; 21, © AP Images/Bill Kostroun; 22, © Andy Manis/Bloomberg News/Landov; 22Logo, © KRT/Newscom.

Publisher: Kenn Goin
Senior Editor: Lisa Wiseman
Creative Director: Spencer Brinker
Photo Researcher: Omni-Photo Communications, Inc.
Design: Dawn Beard Creative

Library of Congress Cataloging-in-Publication Data

Sandler, Michael, 1965–
    Brett Favre / by Michael Sandler.
        p. cm. — (Football heroes making a difference)
    Includes bibliographical references and index.
    ISBN-13: 978-1-59716-771-0 (library binding)
    ISBN-10: 1-59716-771-1 (library binding)
    1. Favre, Brett—Juvenile literature. 2. Football players—United States—Biography—Juvenile literature. 3. Quarterbacks (Football)—United States—Biography—Juvenile literature. 4. Green Bay Packers (Football team)—Juvenile literature. I. Title.

    GV939.F29S26 2009
    796.332092—dc22
    [B]
                                            2008031176

For more information, write to Bearport Publishing Company, Inc., 101 Fifth Avenue, Suite 6R, New York, New York 10003. Printed in the United States of America.

10 9 8 7 6 5 4 3 2 1

CONTENTS

Brett's Big Chance

All Brett wanted was a chance. As an Atlanta Falcons **rookie**, however, he never got one. He barely left the **bench**, throwing just four passes all year.

Then he was traded to Wisconsin's Green Bay Packers. For Brett, it was a brand-new start. On September 20, 1992, during the third game of the season, the Packers' coach, Mike Holmgren, sent him onto the field.

How did the young quarterback do? He **fumbled** four times against the Cincinnati Bengals! Green Bay was losing and Brett was worried. "These fans are going to run me out of town," Brett thought.

Brett spent very little time on the field as an Atlanta Falcon.

Green Bay coach Mike Holmgren talks to Brett on the sidelines during the game against the Bengals.

Brett was **drafted** by the **NFL**'s Atlanta Falcons in 1991. He was traded to Green Bay before the 1992 season.

Coming from Behind

Brett was desperate to earn the fans' cheers and make the most of his opportunity. He didn't have much time, though. With a minute left in the game, the Packers were down by six points. The **end zone** was 90 long yards (82 m) away!

As the seconds ticked down, Brett rocketed the ball to **receiver** Sterling Sharpe for a 42-yard (38-m) gain. Then, with 13 seconds left, Brett passed the ball to receiver Kitrick Taylor for the game-winning touchdown.

Packers fans roared. They would never forget this day, and Brett would never forget the chance he'd been given.

Brett thinks about his next move.

Brett gets ready to throw the ball during the game against the Bengals.

After the Bengals game, Brett became Green Bay's **starting** quarterback.

7

The Boy Who Could Throw

Brett's love for football began when he was a child in Kiln, Mississippi. He grew up in a big house on a dirt road. He loved running through the woods, wrestling with his brothers, and playing any sport where he could throw a ball.

Even when he was young, Brett's arm was amazingly strong. In Little League, some kids cried in fear while waiting to swing at his pitches. Other players refused to bat against him.

Brett could toss a football as hard as he threw a baseball. His passes often left bruises on the chests of kids who caught them.

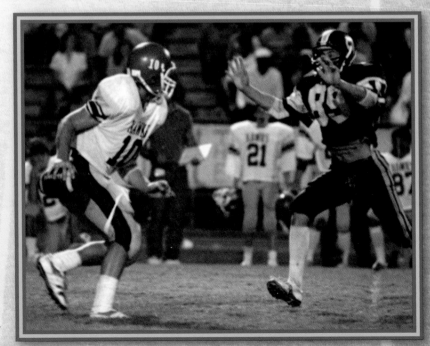

Brett (#10) playing football for his high school team

Brett (top left) and his family

In fifth grade, Brett could already throw 50-yard (46-m) passes!

Southern Mississippi Surprise

After high school, in 1987, Brett headed off to the University of Southern Mississippi. The football team already had six quarterbacks. So when Brett arrived, he was asked to play defense.

On the first day of training camp, coach Jim Carmody was startled by a loud, whooshing sound. The noise was Brett throwing a football. "I'd coached a long time and I never heard a ball sound like that," he recalled.

Coach Carmody quickly decided to give Brett a shot at quarterback. Brett made the most of this opportunity. He took the job and never looked back.

Brett won 29 games in four years at Southern Mississippi.

Brett drops back to throw the ball during a game against Florida State in 1989.

Before his senior year of college, Brett was seriously injured in a car accident. His brother pulled him from the wreck, saving his life. Somehow, Brett quickly recovered and, just five weeks later, led Southern Mississippi to a big win against the University of Alabama.

Winning Fans in Green Bay

After college, Brett was eager to test his skills in the NFL. When Green Bay finally gave him the chance, he was thrilled.

Packers fans were just as happy. They learned to love Brett's bravery—he was never afraid to throw the ball—and his toughness. If Brett had bruised ribs, sprained ankles, or was coughing up blood, he still wanted to be in the game.

Naturally, fans also loved Brett's winning record. In 1993, Green Bay made the playoffs, their first trip in ten years. Then, after the 1995 season, the Packers reached the **NFC Championship Game**.

Green Bay fans cheer on the Packers.

Brett runs with the ball in a playoff win after the 1995 season.

Beginning in 1992, Green Bay went 13 straight years without a **losing season** with Brett as quarterback.

13

Super Bowl Victory!

In 1996, the Packers were unstoppable. Brett took them all the way to Super Bowl XXXI (31) to face the New England Patriots.

New England took an early 14-10 lead. Then Brett and the Packers took over. Early in the second quarter, Brett saw receiver Antonio Freeman speeding down the right side of the field. He lofted the ball to Antonio for an 81-yard (74-m) touchdown.

Green Bay grabbed the lead and never trailed again. They beat the Patriots, 35-21, for their first championship in 30 years.

Brett's 81-yard (74-m) touchdown to Antonio Freeman (#86) was the longest in Super Bowl history.

Brett and a teammate celebrate during Super Bowl XXXI (31).

The Super Bowl win gave Green Bay their 12th league **title**, the most of any NFL team.

Giving Back

Over the years, Brett never forgot the chances he'd been given throughout his career. He wanted to give others the same opportunities to succeed. So in 1996, he started the Brett Favre Fourward **Foundation**. This group focuses on helping **disadvantaged** or **disabled** children in Wisconsin and Mississippi, two special places for Brett.

Brett's goal is to make sure these kids have the chance to lead normal lives. For example, in Green Bay, he helped build a baseball field and playground with special surfaces for children in wheelchairs. The field and playground have changed the lives of many young people. "Before, these kids always had to sit and watch. Now they get to play," said one parent.

Some of Brett's teammates, Johnny Quinn, Desmond Bishop, and Scott Wells, attended opening day at the new field.

Since Brett's foundation began, it has given $4 million to dozens of charities.

Adam, nine years old, at bat on the new baseball field in Green Bay

17

Hometown Helper

Another way Brett helps is by **donating** money to Gaits to Success in Mississippi. This group uses **therapy horses** to help kids facing challenges such as **autism** and **cerebral palsy**. When children with these conditions learn to ride horses, they gain confidence and a new sense of freedom.

In August 2005, Hurricane Katrina swept into Louisiana and Mississippi. The storms **devastated** big cities such as New Orleans and smaller places like Brett's hometown, Kiln. Brett got to work right away. He helped raise hundreds of thousands of dollars to rebuild homes, sports fields, and playgrounds destroyed by the terrible storm.

Destin, a student with Gaits to Success, plays basketball while riding a therapy horse named Rocky.

Brett, First Lady Laura Bush, and some children from Kiln, Mississippi, cut a ribbon during a ceremony celebrating a playground that was built to replace one that was destroyed by Hurricane Katrina.

Brett knew firsthand about the damage Katrina caused. The storm destroyed his childhood home.

Beyond Green Bay

In March 2008, Brett retired after 275 straight games as the Packers' quarterback. For 16 seasons, he had brought joy to fans at Green Bay's Lambeau Field. He'd sometimes play hurt, often led a comeback, and always made spectacular passes.

A few months later, however, Brett changed his mind. He loved football too much to retire. He felt that he still had more to give. Green Bay had moved on, though. They had a new young quarterback, so they traded Brett to the New York Jets.

No one knows how long the 38-year-old quarterback will keep playing. One thing is certain: few athletes have given more on or off the field than Brett Favre.

Brett signs autographs for some Jets fans.

Brett, in a Jets uniform, warms up before a preseason game against the Washington Redskins.

In January 2008, after a superb final season with Green Bay, Brett led the Packers into the NFC Championship Game. Unfortunately, an overtime loss to the New York Giants kept Green Bay out of another Super Bowl.

The Brett File

Brett is a football hero on and off the field. Here are some highlights.

- In 1992, his first season as Green Bay's starting quarterback, Brett was voted onto the NFC **Pro Bowl** team. He became the youngest quarterback ever to play in a Pro Bowl.

- Brett holds many NFL all-time records. At the start of the 2008 season, these included most wins as starting quarterback—160; most touchdown passes—442; and most passing yards—61,655 (56,337 m).

- During Brett's career in Green Bay, he started 253 straight games for the Packers—275 including the playoffs.

- Each year, Brett holds a golf tournament and concert in Mississippi to raise money for his foundation. The 2006 tournament raised more than $400,000.

- Brett's foundation helps many different groups, including the Make-A-Wish Foundation, the Boys and Girls Clubs of America, and the Special Olympics.

Glossary

autism (AW-tiz-uhm) a medical condition that makes it difficult for people to communicate or relate to others

bench (BENCH) seats on the sides of the field where players sit when they're not playing

cerebral palsy (SER-uh-bral PAWL-zee) a medical condition caused by brain damage that makes it hard for people to control their movements

devastated (DEV-uh-*stay*-tid) severely damaged

disabled (diss-AY-buhld) unable to do certain things because of an illness or injury

disadvantaged (diss-uhd-VAN-tijd) poor and lacking many opportunities

donating (DOH-nate-ing) giving something as a gift

drafted (DRAFT-id) chosen or picked to play for a team

end zone (END ZOHN) the area at either end of a football field where touchdowns are scored

foundation (foun-DAY-shuhn) an organization that supports or gives money to worthwhile causes

fumbled (FUHM-buhld) dropped or lost the football during a play

losing season (LOOZ-ing SEE-zuhn) a season in which a team loses more games than it wins

NFC Championship Game (EN EFF SEE CHAM-pee-uhn-*ship* GAME) a playoff game that decides which National Football Conference (NFC) team will go to the Super Bowl

NFL (EN-EFF-ELL) the National Football League

Pro Bowl (PROH BOHL) the yearly all-star game for the season's best NFL players

receiver (ri-SEE-vur) a player whose job it is to catch passes

rookie (RUK-ee) a player who is in his first year of pro football

starting (START-ing) playing at the start of a game; the best player at a position

therapy horses (THER-uh-pee HORSS-iz) horses that are used to help people with disabilities strengthen their muscles and improve their balance and coordination; riding the horses also gives these people a sense of independence

title (TYE-tuhl) the championship

Bibliography

D'Amato, Gary. "Brett Favre: The Making of a Legend." *Milwaukee Journal Sentinel* (9/10/2005–12/31/2005).

Shipnuck, Alan. "A Man In Full." *Sports Illustrated* (March 12, 2008).

www.brettfavre.com

Read More

Frisch, Aaron. *Green Bay Packers: Super Bowl Champions.* Mankato, MN: Creative Education (2005).

Krumenauer, Heidi. *Brett Favre.* Hockessin, DE: Mitchell Lane Publishers (2008).

Stewart, Mark. *The Green Bay Packers.* Chicago, IL: Norwood House Press (2007).

Learn More Online

To learn more about Brett Favre, the Fourward Foundation, the Green Bay Packers, and the New York Jets, visit **www.bearportpublishing.com/FootballHeroes**

Index